D1505320

# Snakes

by Martha E. H. Rustad

Consulting Editor: Gail Saunders-Smith, Ph.D.

Consultant: Jennifer Zablotny, D.V.M.,
Member, American Animal Hospital Association

## Pebble Books

an imprint of Capstone Press
Mankato, Minnesota

Pebble Books are published by Capstone Press
151 Good Counsel Drive, P.O. Box 669, Mankato, Minnesota 56002
http://www.capstone-press.com

1  2  3  4  5  6  07  06  05  04  03  02

*Library of Congress Cataloging-in-Publication Data*
Rustad, Martha E. H. (Martha Elizabeth Hillman), 1975–
    Snakes / by Martha E. H. Rustad.
    p. cm.—All about pets (Mankato, Minn.)
    Includes bibliographical references (p. 23) and index.
    ISBN 0-7368-0977-5
    1. Snakes as pets—Juvenile literature. 2. Snakes—Juvenile literature. [1. Snakes
as pets. 2. Pets.] I. Title. II. All about pets (Mankato, Minn.)
SF459.S5 R87 2002
639.3'96—dc21                                                    2001000260

Summary: Simple text and photographs introduce pet snakes, their features, and
basic care.

# Note to Parents and Teachers

The All About Pets series supports national science standards
for units on the diversity and unity of life. This book describes
domesticated snakes and illustrates what they need from their
owners. The photographs support emergent readers in
understanding the text. The repetition of words and phrases
helps emergent readers learn new words. This book also introduces
emergent readers to subject-specific vocabulary words, which are
defined in the Words to Know section. Emergent readers may need
assistance to read some words and to use the Table of Contents,
Words to Know, Read More, Internet Sites, and Index/Word List
sections of the book.

# Table of Contents

Some snakes are pets.

tongue

Snakes have a tongue.

8

Snakes have scales.

Snakes shed their skin
to grow.

Snakes need water.

14

Snakes need food.

Snakes need
a clean cage.

Snakes need heat.

Snakes need a place
to hide.

# Words to Know

**cage**—a container that holds an animal; snake cages must have a tight cover so pet snakes cannot escape.

**food**—something that people, animals, and plants need to stay alive and grow; some snakes eat mice, rats, eggs, birds, frogs, insects, and other snakes.

**heat**—warmth; snakes need heat to stay warm; pet snake owners should leave a heat lamp on during the day; the lamp should be off at night so snakes can rest in a cool place.

**pet**—a tame animal kept for company or pleasure; only certain kinds of snakes should be kept as pets; wild snakes do not make good pets.

**scale**—one of the small pieces of hard skin that covers the body of a snake or other reptile

**tongue**—the moveable muscle in the mouth; snakes use their tongue to help them smell.

# Read More

**Coborn, John.** *Snakes.* Basic Domestic Reptile and Amphibian Library. Philadelphia: Chelsea House Publishers, 1999.

**Gutman, Bill.** *Becoming Best Friends with Your Iguana, Snake, or Turtle.* Pet Friends. Brookfield, Conn.: Millbrook Press, 2001.

**Silverstein, Alvin, Virginia Silverstein, and Laura Silverstein Nunn.** *Snakes and Such.* What a Pet! Brookfield, Conn.: Twenty-First Century Books, 1999.

# Internet Sites

### Care Sheet for Snakes
http://petstation.com/snakcare.html

### Choosing a Snake
http://petplace.netscape.com/netscape/
nsArtShow.asp?artID=1464

### Snake-Keeping Basics
http://www.petsmart.com/articles/article_7289.shtml

# Index/Word List

**Word Count: 37**
**Early-Intervention Level: 6**

**Credits**

Kia Bielke, cover designer and illustrator; Kimberly Danger, photo researcher

Capstone Press/Laurie Grassel, 1, 4, 6, 8, 10 (both), 12, 14, 16, 18, 20
Visuals Unlimited/Bill Beatty, cover